Book Ends for the Reader

Topic: Fall

Notes to Parents and Teachers:

The books your child reads at this level will have more of a storyline with details to discuss. Have children practice reading more fluently at this level. Take turns reading pages with your child so you can model what fluent reading sounds like.

REMEMBER: PRAISE IS A GREAT MOTIVATOR!

Here are some praise points for beginning readers:

• I love how you read that sentence so it sounded just like you were talking.

• Great job reading that sentence like a question!

• WOW! You read that page with such good expression!

Let's Make Paired Reading Connections:

Trick or Treat

• First, read the fiction text *Trick or Treat* by Robin Wells.

• Next, read the nonfiction text *Celebrations Around the World*.

• What celebrations did you learn about in this book?

• What celebration did you learn about in the storybook?

• Look at the pictures of the celebrations in both books. What do you notice is the same for almost all celebrations?

Table of Contents

Rourke
Educational Media
rourkeeducationalmedia.com

Can you find these words?

celebrate

dragons

masks

powder

Celebrations Around the World

celebrate

People love to **celebrate**.

People in India celebrate spring.

They throw colored **powder** in the air.

powder

People in China also celebrate spring. This is the Chinese New Year.

Look at those **dragons!**

dragons

People in Brazil celebrate Carnival.

8

mask

People wear **masks**.
They dance in the streets.

9

Japan celebrates Children's Day.

People fly banners shaped like fish.

People in many places celebrate Christmas. They give gifts.

They sing songs.
What do you celebrate?

Did you find these words?

People love to **celebrate**.

Look at those **dragons!**

People wear **masks**.

They throw colored **powder** in the air.

Photo Glossary

 **celebrate** (SEL-uh-brate): To do something special to mark a happy time or event.

 **dragons** (DRAG-uhns): Make-believe creatures that breathe fire.

 **masks** (masks): Coverings that hide people's faces.

 **powder** (POU-dur): A dry substance made of tiny, loose particles.

Index

About the Author

Katy Duffield is a writer. Her favorite thing to celebrate is her birthday. She likes to open presents, but her favorite part of celebrating her birthday is eating chocolate cake!

© 2019 Rourke Educational Media

www.rourkeeducationalmedia.com

PHOTO CREDITS: Cover ©triloks, © tsvibrav, Page 2,3,14,15 ©shironosov, Page 4 ©THEPALMER, Page 2,5,14,15 ©Nuno Valadas, Page 2,6-7,14,15 ©aluxum, Page 8 ©SerengetiLion, Page 2,9,14,15 ©Brasil2, Page 10-11 ©akiyoko, Page 12-13 ©kajakiki

Edited by: Keli Sipperley
Cover design by: Kathy Walsh
Interior design by: Kathy Walsh

Library of Congress PCN Data
Celebrations Around the World / Katy Duffield
(Let's Find Out)
ISBN (hard cover)(alk. paper) 978-1-64156-194-5
ISBN (soft cover) 978-1-64156-250-8
ISBN (e-Book) 978-1-64156-300-0
Library of Congress Control Number: 2017957804

Printed in the United States of America, North Mankato, Minnesota